Cinnabunnies

2 c. biscuit baking mix
1/2 c. **Sun-Maid Natural Raisins**
1/2 c. sour cream
3 T. milk
2 T. butter, softened

1/2 c. brown sugar, packed
1/4 c. nuts, finely chopped
1/2 t. cinnamon
Garnish: raisins, sliced almonds

In a bowl, stir together baking mix, raisins, sour cream and milk until just combined. Gently gather dough into a ball on a floured tea towel. Knead 10 times. Roll out dough into a 12-inch by 10-inch rectangle. Spread dough with butter. Mix together brown sugar, nuts and cinnamon; sprinkle over dough. Starting at a long end, roll up dough tightly. Cut roll into 12 slices. Place 6 slices, cut-side down, on a greased baking sheet about 3 inches apart. Unroll remaining 6 rolls and place on cookie sheet touching one of the rolled cinnamon rolls; fold ends under and shape into bunny ears. Pinch dough to secure. Arrange raisins and almonds to look like eyes, noses and teeth. Bake at 400 degrees for 15 minutes, or until golden. Makes 6.

Children are sure to be helpful in the kitchen when they're wearing their very own kid-size aprons. Visit a craft store to select fabric crayons and plain canvas aprons, then let kids decorate their apron as they like. Follow package directions for making the design permanent.

Kid-Friendly Recipes

Raisin Waffle Toast

3 eggs, beaten
3 T. milk
2 T. brown sugar, packed
1/4 t. vanilla extract

6 to 8 slices **Sun-Maid Cinnamon Swirl Raisin Bread**

In a shallow bowl, whisk together eggs, milk, brown sugar and vanilla. Dip bread slices in egg mixture, coating both sides. Place bread slices, one at a time, on a heated non-stick waffle iron. Close lid and cook for 3 minutes, or until golden. Makes 6 to 8 servings.

Yummy pancake and waffle syrup in your favorite fruit flavor! Combine a small box of fruit-flavored gelatin, one cup water, 1/2 cup sugar and 2 tablespoons cornstarch in a saucepan. Bring to a rolling boil, pour into a syrup pitcher and let cool slightly before serving.

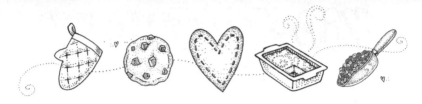

Pumpkin Patch Bread

2 c. sugar
2/3 c. butter, softened
15-oz. can pumpkin
2/3 c. milk
4 eggs, beaten
3-1/3 c. all-purpose flour
2 t. baking soda
1/2 t. baking powder
1-1/2 t. salt
1 t. cinnamon
1 t. ground cloves
2/3 c. **Sun-Maid Natural Raisins**
2/3 c. chopped nuts

Blend sugar and butter in a large bowl; stir in pumpkin, milk and eggs. Set aside. In a separate bowl, combine flour, baking soda, baking powder, salt and spices; stir into pumpkin mixture. Add raisins and nuts. Spoon into 2 greased 8"x4" loaf pans. Bake at 350 degrees for one hour, or until a toothpick comes out clean. Makes 2 loaves.

Throw a pumpkin painting party! Provide acrylic paints, brushes and plenty of pumpkins...invite kids to bring their imagination and an old shirt to wear as a smock. Parents are sure to join in too!

Kid-Friendly Recipes

Cheery Cherry Oatmeal

2-1/2 c. water
1-1/2 c. long-cooking oats, uncooked
1/2 t. cinnamon
1/8 c. **Sun-Maid Golden Raisins**
1/8 c. **Sun-Maid Tart Cherries**
1/4 c. chopped pecans
Garnish: brown sugar, milk

In a large saucepan over high heat, bring water to a boil. Add oats; return to a boil. Cook and stir constantly for one minute; reduce heat. Cover and simmer for 5 minutes, or until water is absorbed, stirring once or twice. Stir in cinnamon, fruit and pecans. Top servings with brown sugar and milk. Serves 6 to 8.

Make school-day breakfasts fun! Cut the centers from a slice of toast with a cookie cutter, serve milk or juice with twisty straws or put a smiley face on a bagel using raisins and cream cheese.

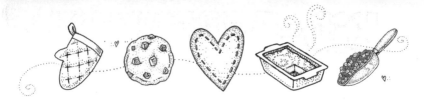

Snappy Sun-Maid Salsa

1/2 c. red pepper, diced
1/2 c. yellow pepper, diced
1/2 c. green pepper, diced
1 c. **Sun-Maid Natural Raisins**, **Apricots** or **Peaches**, chopped
1 c. fresh pineapple, diced
1/2 c. red onion, diced
Optional: 1/2 c. jicama, diced
1/4 c. fresh cilantro or parsley, finely chopped
1/2 jalapeño, seeded and minced
2 to 3 T. lime juice
1 clove garlic, minced
1/2 t. chili powder
1/4 t. ground cumin
1/4 t. salt
tortilla chips

In a bowl, combine all ingredients except tortilla chips; mix well. Cover and refrigerate for at least one hour to allow flavors to blend. Serve with tortilla chips. Makes about 3 cups.

Stack up six or seven little story books of favorite nursery tales and tie them in a bright red ribbon. Drop in the local children's charity toybox...a wonderful gift.

Kid-Friendly Recipes

Grandma's Dressing

3/4 c. onion, chopped
1/2 c. celery, sliced
1 c. butter
14-1/2 oz. can chicken broth
1/2 c. **Sun-Maid Natural Raisins**
8-oz. pkg. herb-flavored stuffing mix
1/3 c. pecans, toasted and coarsely chopped

In a skillet over medium heat, sauté onion and celery in butter until softened, about 2 to 3 minutes. Stir in broth and raisins. Bring to a boil; reduce heat and simmer, uncovered, for 3 minutes. Add in stuffing mix and pecans. Remove from heat; cover and let stand 5 minutes. Fluff with a fork before serving. Makes 6 to 8 servings.

Remember your favorite childhood toys? Many can still be shared with kids today...Mr. Potato Head, Silly Putty, Slinky and Lincoln Logs are fun no matter what your age.

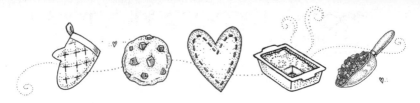

Honey-Nut Stuffed Celery

8-oz. pkg. light cream cheese, softened
1 c. honey
1/4 c. chopped nuts
1/4 c. **Sun-Maid Cape Cod Cranberries**
6 stalks celery, halved crosswise

In a bowl, stir together cream cheese, honey, nuts and cranberries. Spread 2 tablespoons cream cheese mixture onto each stalk of celery. Makes 12 pieces.

Involve kids in mealtime preparation. They can set the table, help with menu selection, pour in the raisins...so much fun!

Kid-Friendly Recipes

Sweet & Savory Yams

2 lbs. yams, peeled and sliced 1/2-inch thick
8-oz. can pineapple chunks, drained and juice reserved
1 apple, cored and cut into 1/2-inch cubes
1/2 c. **Sun-Maid Natural Raisins**
1 T. butter
1 c. onion, thinly sliced
2 T. brown sugar, packed
1/2 t. salt

Combine yams, pineapple and apple in a lightly greased 13"x9" baking pan. Sprinkle raisins over top; set aside. Melt butter in a skillet over medium heat. Add onion and cook, stirring occasionally, until softened and golden. Stir reserved pineapple juice, brown sugar and salt into onion mixture. Cook and stir until sugar is dissolved; pour over yam mixture. Bake, covered in aluminum foil, at 350 degrees for one hour, or until yams are tender. Makes 8 to 10 servings.

Sprinkle crumbled gingersnap cookies over yam and sweet potato casseroles for a sweet, crunchy topping.

Confetti Carrot Salad

1 lb. carrots, peeled and shredded
8-1/4 oz. can crushed pineapple, drained
1/2 c. **Sun-Maid Natural Raisins**
1 t. lemon juice
1 T. honey
2 T. mayonnaise
2 T. sour cream
1/8 t. allspice
Optional: 1/4 c. toasted, chopped pecans,
1/2 c. mini marshmallows

In a bowl, mix together carrots, pineapple and raisins. In a separate bowl, whisk together lemon juice, honey, mayonnaise, sour cream and allspice until well blended. Pour over carrot mixture; mix well. Chill for at least one hour to allow flavors to blend. Just before serving, fold in pecans and marshmallows, if using. Serves 4 to 6.

Make store-bought coleslaw your own by adding shredded Cheddar cheese, apple, bell pepper or raisins.

KID-FRIENDLY Recipes

Fruited Chinese Chicken Salad

2 c. cooked chicken, chopped
8-oz. can sliced water chestnuts, drained
1 c. **Sun-Maid Natural Raisins**
1 c. celery, sliced
1/2 c. carrot, peeled and thinly sliced
1/2 c. slivered almonds, toasted
1/4 c. green onion, sliced
1 head Chinese cabbage, chopped

In a large bowl, combine all ingredients except cabbage; drizzle with Dressing. Toss mixture to coat. Serve over chopped cabbage. Serves 6.

Dressing:

1/4 c. cider vinegar
2 T. soy sauce
2 T. oil
2 T. sugar
1 clove garlic, minced

Whisk together all ingredients in a bowl.

If there's leftover chopped salad after dinner, use it for a tasty sandwich filling the next day. Split a pita round, stuff with salad and drizzle with salad dressing...yummy!

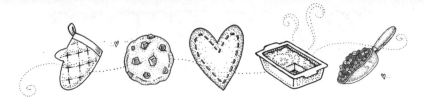

Car-Tuna Take-Alongs

1/2 c. low-fat mayonnaise
1/2 c. low-fat plain yogurt
Optional: 1-1/2 t. curry
 powder
1 c. **Sun-Maid Natural
 Raisins** or **Fruit Bits**
1/2 c. celery or red or green
 pepper, diced
1 green onion, thinly sliced
12-oz. can tuna, drained
6 small round or oval
 sandwich rolls

In a bowl, combine mayonnaise, yogurt and curry powder, if using. Stir in raisins or fruit bits, celery or pepper and green onion; fold in tuna. Cut a 1/2-inch slice off the top of each roll. Hollow out rolls, reserving bread crumbs for another use. Fill each roll with 1/2 cup tuna mixture; replace roll tops. Makes 6 sandwiches.

Turn your Car-Tuna sandwiches into fun works of art! Using toothpicks to hold everything in place, turn them into cars by using dried apricots and raisins for wheels, dried apple slices for fenders and raisins or dried cherries for headlights. Or why not turn them into silly bears by using dried apricots for ears, raisins or dried cherries for eyes, a prune for a nose and a dried apple slice for a big smile...cute!

Kid-Friendly Recipes

Apple-Stuffed Pork Chops

6 thick-cut pork chops
salt and pepper to taste
1-1/2 c. toasted bread crumbs
1/2 c. apple, cored and chopped
1/2 c. shredded sharp Cheddar cheese
2 T. **Sun-Maid Natural Raisins**
2 T. butter, melted
2 T. orange juice
1/4 t. salt
1/8 t. cinnamon

Cut a pocket into the side of each pork chop; sprinkle pockets with salt and pepper. Set aside. Toss bread crumbs, apple, cheese and raisins together; set aside. Combine butter, orange juice, salt and cinnamon; stir into apple mixture. Stuff pockets with mixture; place in an ungreased 13"x9" baking pan. Bake, uncovered, at 350 degrees for 15 minutes; cover. Bake for an additional 15 minutes, or until pork is cooked through. Makes 6 servings.

Cut sandwiches with cookie cutters for lunch box treats... your kids will think you hung the moon and stars!

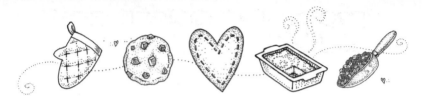

No-Hurry Chicken Curry

2 T. olive oil
3-lbs. chicken, skin removed
2 cloves garlic, minced
1 onion, chopped
1 green pepper, chopped
1/2 c. celery, chopped
2 t. curry powder
1/3 c. **Sun-Maid Natural Raisins**
14-1/2 oz. can whole tomatoes, chopped
1 t. sugar
salt and pepper to taste
cooked rice
Garnish: 1/4 c. slivered almonds

Heat oil in a skillet over medium heat. Sauté chicken just until golden; place in a slow cooker and set aside. Add garlic, onion, green pepper, celery and curry powder to skillet; sauté briefly. Remove from heat; stir in remaining ingredients except rice and almonds. Pour over chicken. Cover and cook on low setting for 6 hours. Serve over cooked rice; sprinkle with almonds. Makes 4 servings.

Just for fun, play "Waiter and Waitress" and let the kids help out in the kitchen...Mom & Dad can be the customers!

Kid-Friendly Recipes

Cool Turkey Pitas

2 c. cooked turkey, chopped
1/2 c. celery, diced
1/2 c. red apple, peeled, cored and diced
1/3 c. **Sun-Maid Natural Raisins**
1/3 c. low-fat plain yogurt
salt and pepper to taste
6 leaves lettuce
3 6-inch pita rounds, halved

Combine turkey, celery, apple, raisins and yogurt in a bowl; season with salt and pepper. Place one leaf lettuce in each pita half. Evenly divide turkey mixture among pita halves. Makes 6 servings.

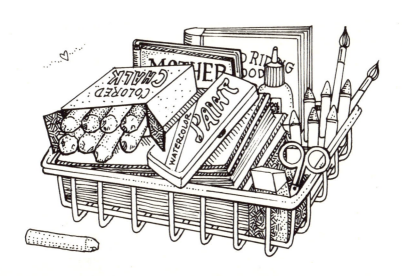

Use a dish drainer to organize children's activity or coloring books. The silverware holders can be used for holding crayons, pencils or pens.

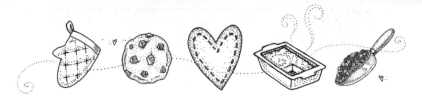

Honey Chicken & Stuffing

3 c. herb-flavored stuffing mix
1 c. hot water
1/2 c. **Sun-Maid Golden Raisins**
2 T. butter, melted
6 boneless, skinless chicken breasts

1/2 c. honey
1/3 c. mayonnaise
1/3 c. Dijon mustard
1/2 t. dried parsley

Combine stuffing, water, raisins and butter; toss to mix and let stand for 3 minutes. Spoon stuffing mixture into 6 mounds in a lightly greased 13"x9" baking pan. Place one chicken breast on top of each mound. Mix together remaining ingredients; spoon over chicken. Cover with aluminum foil. Bake at 400 degrees for 25 to 30 minutes. Remove foil and bake for an additional 5 minutes, or until golden and chicken juices run clear. Serves 6.

An edible, glittery garnish...roll grapes, strawberries and blueberries in extra-fine sugar. Kids will eat 'em up!

Kid-Friendly Recipes

Just-Perfect Margherita Pizza Pie

2 T. olive oil
1 clove garlic, minced
12-inch Italian pizza crust
2 to 3 Roma tomatoes, thinly sliced
1/3 c. **Sun-Maid Natural Raisins**
2 T. fresh basil, thinly sliced
1/2 c. shredded mozzarella cheese
1/4 c. shredded Parmesan cheese
salt to taste

In a small bowl, whisk together olive oil and garlic; spread over pizza crust. Arrange tomato slices over crust; sprinkle with raisins, basil and cheeses. Season with salt. Bake at 350 degrees for 15 to 18 minutes, until cheese is melted and crust is crisp. Makes 4 servings.

Kids will feel extra-special when served sparkling grape juice or cranberry juice cocktail in long-stemmed plastic glasses.

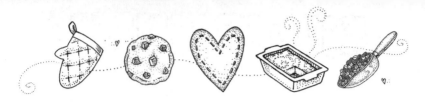

Monte Cristo Sandwiches

4 t. honey Dijon mustard
8 slices **Sun-Maid Cinnamon Swirl Raisin Bread**
8 slices Swiss cheese
8 slices deli ham
2 eggs, beaten
2 T. all-purpose flour
1 T. butter, melted
1/4 t. salt
1/4 t. pepper
2 T. milk

Spread 1/2 teaspoon mustard on each slice of bread. On one slice of bread, layer one slice of cheese, one slice of ham and another slice of cheese; top with another slice of bread. Repeat for remaining 3 sandwiches. In a bowl, whisk together remaining ingredients. Dip both sides of sandwiches into egg mixture; place on a lightly greased baking sheet. Drizzle with any remaining egg mixture. Bake at 425 degrees for 8 to 10 minutes, until tops are golden. Flip sandwiches over and bake for an additional 8 to 10 minutes, until both sides are golden. Makes 4 sandwiches.

National Sandwich Day is November 3rd...celebrate and serve up a favorite sandwich!

Kid-Friendly Recipes

Picadillo Wraps

1 T. oil
1 lb. ground beef
1 onion, chopped
4 cloves garlic, minced
2 t. chili powder
2 t. ground cumin
1 t. salt
1/4 t. cinnamon
3/4 c. instant rice, uncooked
2 14-1/2 oz. cans Mexican-style diced tomatoes
1/2 c. salsa
3/4 c. **Sun-Maid Natural Raisins**
16-oz. can black beans, drained
flour tortillas
Optional: chopped fresh cilantro, shredded Cheddar cheese, sour cream

Heat oil in a large skillet over medium heat. Add beef, onion and garlic to oil; season with chili powder, cumin, salt and cinnamon. Cook and stir until browned; drain. Stir in rice, tomatoes with juice, salsa and raisins; bring to a simmer. Cover and cook for 10 minutes, or until rice is tender. Stir in beans. Cover and cook for 5 minutes, or until heated through. Serve wrapped in warm tortillas with cilantro, cheese and sour cream, if using. Makes 6 servings.

When the kids study another country in school, why not try out a treat from that country? Let them help choose a recipe and shop for the ingredients...they'll learn so much and have fun doing it!

Stuffed Banana Smiles

1 banana, unpeeled
1 T. **Sun-Maid Natural Raisins** or **Golden Raisins**

1 T. semi-sweet, milk or white chocolate chips

Place banana flat on its side on a microwave-safe plate. Starting and ending 1/4-inch from the ends of banana, slice open lengthwise while also slicing the banana inside. Carefully open banana wide enough to sprinkle raisins and chocolate chips inside. Microwave banana, uncovered, on high for 40 to 60 seconds, until chocolate begins to melt and banana is still firm. Serve immediately, scooping with a spoon right out of the banana peel. Makes one serving.

Remember the fun of digging down in a box of caramel corn and peanuts for the little prize? Make some homemade snack mix and pack it up in individual Chinese takeout cartons, wrap little toys and treasures in wax paper and hide them in the cartons!

Kid-Friendly Recipes

Spooky Spiders

creamy peanut butter
buttery round crackers

pretzel sticks
Sun-Maid Natural Raisins

For each spider, spread peanut butter on a cracker, place 4 pretzel sticks on each side for "legs." Spread peanut butter on a second cracker and press together gently. Use a little peanut butter to stick 2 raisin "eyes" to top of cracker. Make as many as you like!

Stir up some old-fashioned fun this Halloween. Light the house with spooky candlelight and serve homemade popcorn balls, pumpkin cookies and hot cider. Bob for apples and play pin the tail on the black cat...kids from 6 to 76 will love it!

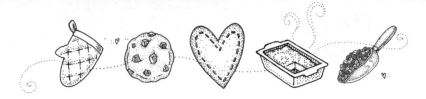

Maple Popcorn Balls

6 T. unpopped popcorn kernels, popped or 2 bags microwave popcorn, popped
2 c. **Sun-Maid Golden Raisins**
2 c. chopped nuts
2/3 c. maple syrup
1-1/2 t. maple extract
2/3 c. apple juice
1/2 c. butter, sliced
3/4 t. salt
2 c. sugar

Combine popcorn, raisins and nuts in a large bowl; set aside. Mix remaining ingredients in a large heavy saucepan. Cook and stir over medium heat until sugar dissolves. If mixture begins to rise above pan, lower heat. Watch closely, as temperature will rise very quickly towards the end. Stop stirring just before mixture reaches hard-crack stage, or 290 to 310 degrees on a candy thermometer. Immediately remove from heat and pour over popcorn mixture; stir to coat. Working quickly with buttered hands, form into tennis ball-sized balls. Cool; wrap in cellophane. Makes about one dozen.

Popcorn ball funny faces! Set out a variety of small candies like gumdrops, candy corn, candy-coated chocolates and licorice whips. Kids can have fun using dabs of marshmallow creme or frosting to make their own creations.

Kid-Friendly Recipes

Tropical Tortilla Wheels

2 T. pineapple cream cheese spread
8-inch flour tortilla
1/2 carrot, peeled and shredded

3 T. **Sun-Maid Tropical Trio or Fruit Bits**

Spread pineapple cream cheese evenly onto one side of tortilla. Sprinkle carrot and Tropical Trio evenly over cream cheese. Roll up tortilla tightly and slice into 8 equal sections. Makes 8 servings.

Stir up some Grizzly Gorp (short for "good old raisins and peanuts") for snacking...just toss together 2 cups bear-shaped graham crackers, 1 cup mini marshmallows, 1 cup peanuts and 1/2 cup raisins. Yum!

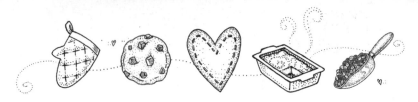

Raisin-Oatmeal Pizza Cookie

3/4 c. butter, softened
1 c. brown sugar, packed
1/2 c. sugar
1/4 c. milk
1 egg
1 t. vanilla extract
1 c. all-purpose flour
1 t. cinnamon
1/2 t. baking soda
1/2 t. salt
3 c. long-cooking oats, uncooked
1 c. **Sun-Maid Natural Raisins**
1-1/2 c. white chocolate chips
Garnish: **Sun-Maid Dried Apricots, Fruit Bits** and **Tropical Trio**

In a bowl, beat together butter, sugars, milk, egg and vanilla until well blended. Beat in flour, cinnamon, baking soda and salt; fold in oats and raisins. Divide dough in half. Pat each half into a 9-inch round on a baking sheet. Bake at 325 degrees for 18 to 20 minutes, or until golden; let cool. Place chocolate chips in a microwave-safe bowl. Microwave for one minute, stirring occasionally, until melted. Spread chocolate over cookies; top with apricots and fruit bits. Press toppings into chocolate to secure; cut into wedges. Makes 2 cookie pizzas; each serves 8.

Plump up raisins for extra moist, tender cookies! Soak them in warm water for 3 to 5 minutes, then drain before adding to recipe.

Kid-Friendly Recipes

Ooey-Gooey Baked Apples

6 Gala or Jonagold apples, cored
1/4 c. butter, softened
1/4 c. brown sugar, packed
1/4 c. maple syrup
1 t. cinnamon
1/2 c. **Sun-Maid Natural Raisins**
1/2 c. walnuts, finely chopped
Garnish: caramel ice cream topping

Arrange cored apples in a lightly greased 13"x9" baking pan and set aside. Combine butter, brown sugar, maple syrup and cinnamon in a small bowl; stir in raisins and walnuts. Spoon mixture into center of apples; cover with aluminum foil. Bake at 325 degrees for one hour, or until apples are tender. Serve warm with caramel topping. Makes 6 servings.

Family night! Serve a simple supper, then spend the evening playing favorite board games or assembling jigsaw puzzles together.

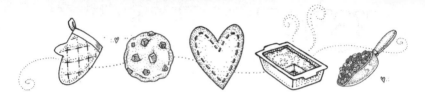

Yummy Spice Cupcakes

2 c. all-purpose flour
1 t. baking soda
1/2 t. baking powder
1/2 t. cinnamon
1 t. pumpkin pie spice
1/2 t. salt

1 c. sugar
1/2 c. butter, melted
15-oz. jar applesauce
1/2 c. **Sun-Maid Natural Raisins**

In a bowl, combine flour, baking soda, baking powder, spices and salt. Stir in sugar and butter. Mix in applesauce until well combined. Stir in raisins. Fill greased muffin cups 2/3 full. Bake at 350 degrees for 20 to 25 minutes, until a toothpick tests clean. Cool completely. Frost with Vanilla Butter Cream Frosting. Makes 1-1/2 dozen.

Vanilla Butter Cream Frosting:

1/2 c. butter, softened
4 c. powdered sugar
1/2 t. salt

1/3 c. milk
1 t. vanilla extract

In a large bowl, beat butter until smooth. Add remaining ingredients; mix until smooth and creamy.

Before adding to cupcake batter, toss nuts, raisins, dried or fresh fruit in flour...it keeps them from sinking to the bottom of the cake!

Kid-Friendly Recipes

Mixed Berry Raisin Cobbler

24-oz. pkg. frozen mixed berries, thawed
1/2 c. sugar
1 T. cornstarch
3/4 c. whole-wheat flour
1/4 c. all-purpose flour
2 T. plus 2 t. sugar, divided
1-1/2 t. baking powder
1/4 t. salt
3/4 c. plus 1/3 c. **Sun-Maid Natural Raisins**, divided
1/3 c. fat-free vanilla yogurt
2 T. butter, melted
1 egg, beaten
Optional: fat-free vanilla frozen yogurt

In a bowl, stir together berries, 1/2 cup sugar and cornstarch. Spoon berry mixture into a lightly greased 11"x7" glass baking pan. Microwave, covered, on high setting for 10 to 12 minutes, stirring twice, until fruit is hot and beginning to thicken. In a small bowl, stir together flours, 2 tablespoons sugar, baking powder and salt. Stir in 3/4 cup raisins; set aside. In a separate small bowl, combine yogurt, butter and egg. Add yogurt mixture to flour mixture; stir until just moistened. Drop biscuit dough by teaspoonfuls over fruit mixture; sprinkle with 2 teaspoons sugar. Bake at 400 degrees for 12 to 14 minutes, until topping is golden; cool slightly. Serve with frozen yogurt, if desired. Makes 8 servings.

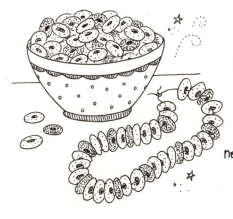

Set little ones down with a bowl of fruit-flavored cereal rings and a long piece of dental floss... they can make cereal necklaces (and nibble away!) while you're baking.

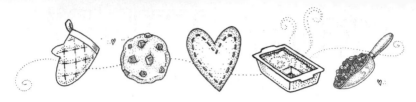

Choco-Raisin Fudge

12-oz. pkg. semi-sweet
  chocolate chips
1 c. crunchy peanut butter

3 c. mini marshmallows
3/4 c. **Sun-Maid Natural Raisins**

Melt chocolate chips and peanut butter in a saucepan over low heat. Fold in marshmallows and raisins; stir until marshmallows are melted. Pour into a greased 11"x7" baking pan; chill until firm. Cut into squares. Store in a cool, dry place. Makes 2 to 3 dozen pieces.

Wrapped in love! Use children's drawings as wrapping paper for gifts from the kitchen. Perfect for grandparents and aunts & uncles.

Kid-Friendly Recipes

Peanutty Raisin Drops

1/2 c. butter, softened
1/2 c. creamy peanut butter
1/2 c. sugar
1/2 c. brown sugar, packed
1 egg
1-2/3 c. all-purpose flour
3/4 t. baking soda
1/2 t. baking powder
1/4 t. salt
1 c. **Sun-Maid Baking Raisins**

In a bowl, mix butter, peanut butter, sugars and egg. Beat until well blended; set aside. In a separate bowl, combine flour, baking soda, baking powder and salt; stir into butter mixture. Mix in raisins. Drop dough by tablespoonfuls onto ungreased baking sheets. Bake at 350 degrees for 12 to 15 minutes. Remove cookies to wire racks to cool. Makes about 3 dozen.

Rolling dough into cookie-size balls is child's play... perfect for kids learning to bake. Make a sample dough ball so they'll know what size to make, set out baking sheets and let the kids take over!

Dorothy's Apricot Strudel

2 c. all-purpose flour
1/2 c. butter, softened
1 c. sour cream
1-1/2 c. **Sun-Maid Dried Apricots,** chopped
1 c. apricot jam
1 c. sweetened flaked coconut
1 c. chopped walnuts
juice of one lemon
Garnish: powdered sugar

In a large bowl, stir together flour, butter and sour cream until a soft dough forms. Wrap dough in plastic wrap and refrigerate for 4 hours to overnight. In a saucepan over low heat, combine apricots, jam, coconut, walnuts and lemon juice. Cook and stir until jam melts and mixture is blended. Remove from heat and set aside. Divide dough equally into 4 pieces. On a floured surface, roll one piece of dough into a 12-inch by 8-inch rectangle. Spread 1/4 of the fruit filling down the center of the dough. Fold sides of dough over filling; invert onto a baking sheet and tuck ends under. Repeat with remaining dough pieces and filling. Bake at 350 degrees for 30 to 35 minutes, until strudels are golden. Cool; sprinkle with powdered sugar. Slice into one-inch strips to serve. Makes 4 strudels.

Applesauce can be used as a fat-free substitute for oil when baking cakes, muffins and other moist, cake-like goods. Just substitute the same amount of applesauce as the recipe calls for oil.

Kid-Friendly Recipes

Mix-in-Pan Fruit Brownies

1 c. sugar
1/2 c. all-purpose flour
6 T. baking cocoa
1/2 c. butter, melted and slightly cooled

2 eggs, beaten
1/2 c. **Sun-Maid Tart Cherries** or **Cape Cod Cranberries**

Stir together sugar, flour and cocoa in an ungreased 8"x8" baking pan; set aside. In a bowl, whisk together butter and eggs. Stir butter mixture into sugar mixture; blend well. Stir in fruit. Bake at 350 degrees for 25 minutes, or until a toothpick inserted in the center tests clean. Cool completely and cut into squares. Makes one dozen.

Take time to share an icy glass of milk and a favorite treat with the kids after school...it's a terrific way to catch up and make sweet memories.

Index

Apple-Stuffed Pork Chops, 13
Car-Tuna Take-Alongs, 12
Cheery Cherry Oatmeal, 5
Choco-Raisin Fudge, 28
Cinnabunnies, 2
Confetti Carrot Salad, 10
Cool Turkey Pitas, 15
Dorothy's Apricot Strudel, 30
Fruited Chinese Chicken Salad, 11
Grandma's Dressing, 7
Honey Chicken & Stuffing, 16
Honey-Nut Stuffed Celery, 8
Just-Perfect Margherita Pizza Pie, 17
Maple Popcorn Balls, 22
Mixed Berry Raisin Cobbler, 27
Mix-in-Pan Fruit Brownies, 31
Monte Cristo Sandwiches, 18
No-Hurry Chicken Curry, 14
Ooey-Gooey Baked Apples, 25
Peanutty Raisin Drops, 29
Picadillo Wraps, 19
Pumpkin Patch Bread, 4
Raisin-Oatmeal Pizza Cookie, 24
Raisin Waffle Toast, 3
Snappy Sun-Maid Salsa, 6
Spooky Spiders, 21
Stuffed Banana Smiles, 20
Sweet & Savory Yams, 9
Tropical Tortilla Wheels, 23
Yummy Spice Cupcakes, 26

U.S. to Metric Recipe Equivalents

Volume Measurements

1/4 teaspoon	1 mL
1/2 teaspoon	2 mL
1 teaspoon	5 mL
1 tablespoon = 3 teaspoons	15 mL
2 tablespoons = 1 fluid ounce	30 mL
1/4 cup	60 mL
1/3 cup	75 mL
1/2 cup = 4 fluid ounces	125 mL
1 cup = 8 fluid ounces	250 mL
2 cups = 1 pint = 16 fluid ounces	500 mL
4 cups = 1 quart	1 L

Weights

1 ounce	30 g
4 ounces	120 g
8 ounces	225 g
16 ounces = 1 pound	450 g

Oven Temperatures

300° F	150° C
325° F	160° C
350° F	180° C
375° F	190° C
400° F	200° C
450° F	230° C

Baking Pan Sizes

Square
8x8x2 inches — 2 L = 20x20x5 cm
9x9x2 inches — 2.5 L = 23x23x5 cm

Rectangular
13x9x2 inches — 3.5 L = 33x23x5 cm

Loaf
9x5x3 inches — 2 L = 23x13x7 cm

Round
8x1-1/2 inches — 1.2 L = 20x4 cm
9x1-1/2 inches — 1.5 L = 23x4 cm